D0948156

APOSTOLIC DOCTRINE
AND
PRACTICE

APOSTOLIC DOCTRINE AND PRACTICE

2nd Edition

KARL FRANKLIN SMITH

ALPHA OMEGA
PUBLISHING

Published in the United States by
Alpha Omega Publishing Company
322 Madison Street, Jackson, MI 49202

Library of Congress Control Number: 2018935630

ISBN: 978-0-9985799-8-6

All Scripture quotations are derived from the Holy Bible, King James Version and New King James Version.

Alpha Omega Publishing Company publishes books that promote the discussion and understanding of the Pentecostal movement throughout the world since the Day of Pentecost. These books are made possible by the enthusiasm of our readers; the support of a committed group of donors, large and small; the collaboration of our many partners in independent media and ecclesiastical organizations; booksellers, who often hand-sell Alpha Omega Publishing books; librarians; and above all by our authors.

Books may be purchased in quantity and/or special sales by contacting the publisher:

Alpha Omega Publishing
E: info@omegapublishing.org
517-879-1286
www.omegapublishing.org

Printed in the United States of America

This book is dedicated to the men and women who are serious about hearing and obeying the word of God and living out the essence of what it means to be a follower of our Lord and Savior, Jesus Christ.

CONTENTS

FOREWORD

If Christian ministers really believe that Christian doctrine is only an intellectual game for theologians and has no bearing upon human life, then it is no wonder that their congregations are ignorant, bored, and bewildered.

The immense value of church history and doctrine is the dimension of historical depth that gives one understanding of the faith and the balance it brings to one's judgement. Some avoid doctrine. They say that it brings contention and broken fellowship and as a result, they do not study or discuss biblical doctrines. However, the Bible is completely filled with doctrines, so one cannot read or teach anything from it without promoting a doctrine. The very word doctrine means "a teaching". We are commanded to "take heed" and "to continue in doctrine" (1 Timothy 4:16). Due to the wide range of thoughts on the subject, this book is not intended for everyone, but it is for the open hearts and minds that are clear of padlocks and prejudices. It is for those who honestly and truly mean business with God. *Apostolic Doctrine and Practice* may test one's sincerity and honesty to no small degree, but a genuine hunger and desire to know the Lord's full thoughts will sustain a careful reading to the end; after which, I say, read it again.

Do not attempt to study this book in a hypothetical way; study it! Use it in your Sunday school classes and Bible studies. Use it to attack sin where it hurts because time is running out and the Lord is soon to come.

Howard Collier

INTRODUCTION

"Whom shall he teach knowledge? and whom shall he make to understand doctrine?" (Isaiah 28:9). Doctrine at its broadest is a set of ideas that are taught or believed to be true. Doctrine differs from theology. The term theology does not appear in the Bible. Theology comes from two Greek words *theos*, meaning "God", and *logos*, meaning "word". Essentially, it means "the word about God" or the common definition, "the study of God". Doctrine originates from the Latin word *doctrina*, which means "teaching" or "instruction". This teaching or instruction can apply to a number of things, but in this case, we will look at it from a Christian viewpoint. The word doctrine is used 56 times in the Bible, occurring 51 in the New Testament. The two Greek words used for doctrine in the New Testament are *didaktos* and *didache*. Both terms mean teaching or instruction in their Latin translation. Hence, doctrine indicates the teaching of God's word, the Bible.

Some Christians view the word doctrine almost as a blasphemous term. The broader philosophy is doctrine should be avoided because it causes division among Christians, and God desires Christians to be united as it is written (John 17:21). While it is true that doctrine causes division, if the division is due to a disagreement over an important biblical instruction, then division is inevitable. The apostle Paul declared, there will come a time when people will no longer listen to sound doctrine and sensible instruction. They will yield to their own desires and will seek out teachers that cater to those desires (2 Timothy 4:3). Further, Scripture says,

"Holding fast the faithful word as he hath been taught, that he may be able by sound doctrine both to exhort and to convince the gainsayers" (Titus 1:9). Essentially, he is recommending teaching sound doctrine and rebuking those who contradict it.

Scripture says the Word of God is profitable for doctrine (2 Timothy 3:16). In the words of Jesus Christ, my doctrine is not mine, but from Him that sent me. The man Jesus was sent by God from above (John 8:23). "If any man will do His will, He shall know of the doctrine, whether it be of God or whether I speak of myself" (John 7:16-17).

It's true that people view and understand the Bible differently. Therefore, different people and church organizations have wavering doctrinal positions. According to Pew Research Center, there are three major Christian denominations in the United States: evangelical Protestantism, mainline Protestantism, and the Catholic Church. There are other Christian denominations that do not fall within any of these groups, such as Eastern Orthodoxy. Why is the philosophy of doctrine so controversial and so important to many people that they will fight, suffer, and make enormous sacrifices when they feel their chosen doctrine is at stake? The reason is because it plays a significant role in various communities and shapes the lives of many individuals. It is no wonder that doctrinal positions are so controversial. The essence of this book is not focused on opposing doctrinal viewpoints of different Christian denominations or establishing new findings for the three major denominations to agree upon. *Apostolic Doctrine and Practice* is focused on the apostles' writings, teachings, and actions in furthering the gospel of Jesus Christ.

Eric A. Beda

~1~

WHAT DID THE APOSTLES BELIEVE?

"Verily, verily, I say unto you, He that believeth on me, the works that I do shall he do also; and greater works than these shall he do".

John 14:12

BELIEVE IN ME

The apostles believed, preached, and taught the words of Jesus. The substance of this book deals with various matters that are somewhat controversial. While I do not delight in controversy, to be faithful in my calling I must, at times, come into conflict with opinions that are contrary to the word of the Lord. God forbid that some would be so averse to differences of opinions that they shun declaring the whole counsel of God.

Why are there so many different denominations amongst Christian worshippers? All of them profess to be worshipping the same Lord, yet they are divergent from one another. Such diversity in denomination presents a mystery to many onlookers. Now, some Christians are seriously concerned about the situation, and have advocated remedies such as the incorporation of all protestant denominations into one giant merger. I'm afraid that would not be the answer and likewise would not be the prescription for solving the dilemma. The lives of the people who make up the congregation are what counts with God. Even if that giant merger were effective, the same ills would still be with us. The protestant group, the Roman Catholic belief, and the Greek Orthodox Church would still exist. Singling out groups is not always wise, but sometimes it is absolutely necessary to be specific. Those three major groups would still be here and the chasm between them would be impossible to bridge.

THE CHURCH

The common theme throughout the 2,000 years since Jesus founded his Church is the church-split phenomenon. The Roman Catholic Church claims all Protestants originated from the Catholic faith, for all Protestants came out of Rome. Five centuries ago, the dominant branch of the traditional Christian religion, the Roman Catholic Church, faced a significant schism as one of its priests and theologians, Martin Luther, rejected several teachings and practices of the church. Among the disputed teachings, Luther strongly opposed the Catholic view on indulgences and that freedom from God's punishment for sin could be purchased with money. The year 2017 marks the 500th anniversary of Martin Luther's *Ninety-Five Theses*, which tradition claims was affixed to the door of the castle church of Wittenberg on October 31, 1517. The *Theses* launched what would become known as the Protestant Reformation. Luther was later excommunicated, and his *Theses* rejected by Pope Leo X in 1520. This split in Christianity was the second major breakup after the Orthodox split of the 11th century[1].

As for the origin of Christianity, please remember that all Christian organizations on the face of the earth originated from Jerusalem. They all came from The Church that was established by Jesus Christ on the Day of Pentecost (Matthew 16:18; Acts 1:8; Acts 2). Rome did not become the center of

---

[1] Luther, M. (2016). *Freedom of a Christian, 1520: The Annotated Luther, Study Edition.* Minneapolis, MN: Fortress Press.

religious worship until about three hundred years later[2]. Therefore, the center of Christian worship was in Jerusalem and it remained there until Jerusalem was destroyed by Titus, the Roman emperor. Therefore, a merger would not be the cure.

If we actually went back to following the teachings of the Roman Catholic Church, and not living in accordance with God's Holy Word, certain harms would still persist. Our condition would be likened to that which was described by the prophet Isaiah: "From the sole of the foot even unto the head there is no soundness in it; but wounds and bruises and putrifying sores: they have not been closed, neither bound up, neither mollified with ointment" (Isaiah 1:6). We would indeed still be sick. It is dangerous to prescribe a remedy for an illness before a proper diagnosis. I believe the ills that are encountered in Christendom are expressed in Isaiah 53:6: "All we like sheep have gone astray; we have turned everyone to his own way." This is our problem. All of our denominations began in Jerusalem on the Day of Pentecost with the outpouring of the Holy Spirit when those present "…began to speak with other tongues as the Spirit of God gave utterance" (Acts 2:1-4). If we find ourselves on different pathways today, it is because as Isaiah said, we have gone astray and have turned each one to his own way. A merger would not cure our ills because if this great merger of souls did not obey the voice of the Lord, it would only be one great conglomeration of people—out of harmony and out of touch with God.

If there is to be a remedy for our ills, we must go back from whence we came. If we have wandered, let's get back on the right track. If we have left the highway of holiness to travel aimlessly from place to place in little detours and

---

[2] Herman, H. L. (2017). *Fundamentals of Pentecostal Oneness.* Jackson, MI: Alpha Omega Publishing Company.

bypaths of sin, selfishness, and carnal opinion, then we shall never make it to our destination—heaven. The only sensible thing for us to do is to get back on the road and go back to the highway. We have departed from the faith which was once delivered to the saints, and today, there are a multitude of faiths, each one of a separate way.

There is but one faith, and I do not need to name it. I know that selfishly each denomination would say that it is their faith and would want it called by a denominational name, but there is no need to put a name or tag on it. Why? Because the Bible profoundly identifies it as "the faith which was once delivered unto the saints" (Jude 1:3).

In the book of Hosea, specifically the sixth chapter, the prophet exhorted Israel to return to the Lord. Israel was prone to wander from God and what He required of them. God would set up certain laws because of the full covenant He had with them, but they would not keep them. They just wandered away. When they found themselves in difficulty, Hosea pleaded with them, "Come, and let us return unto the Lord: for he hath torn and he will heal us; he hath smitten, and he will bind us up" (Hosea 6:1). If there is to be a cure for our mischiefs, it is in returning to God. On one occasion, when Israel was trying to figure out what they might do to deliver themselves, and what alliances they would make with the heathen nations around them, the prophet Jeremiah repeated, "In returning and rest shall ye be saved; in quietness and in confidence shall be your strength" (Isaiah 30:15). If we want to be healed from the problems that plague Christendom, then it behooves those of us who call ourselves by the name of Jesus Christ to awake and find out just how far we have strayed from the original landmark. We must all dedicate ourselves to returning to doing as was done in the days of the apostles. The remedy for our problems is available to all that genuinely seek for it; its confines are found in the doctrine and practices of the apostles.

THE APOSTLE JAMES

Some object to this reference to the apostles, saying, "Who were the apostles? They were just men." Well, dear reader, I will grant that yes, they were men, but they were not just men. They were men who God called, tutored, and endued with power to be witnesses for Jesus Christ "... in Jerusalem, and in all Judaea, and in Samaria, and unto the uttermost part of the earth" (Acts 1:8). They were men who God had uniquely placed, qualified and established in the body. Paul declared in his letter to the Ephesians, "And he gave some, apostles; and some, prophets; and some, evangelists; and some, pastors and teachers; For the perfecting of the saints, for the work of the ministry, for the edifying of the body of Christ" (4:11-12). He set some in the body, first apostles, then prophets, then pastors, and evangelists, and teachers. What for? "For the perfecting of the saints, for the work of the ministry, for the edifying of the body of Christ."

The position of apostle was established in the genesis of church history for the perfecting of the church and because they were so ordained. Hence, we would do well to return to their doctrine and practices. Yet, as men, they were still capable of committing errors. Recorded in the fifteenth chapter of the Acts of the Apostles, a council session that was held in Jerusalem concerning the lifestyle choices of a great number of Gentiles was filled with the Holy Spirit. A doctrinal conference had been convened because some of the saved Jews complained that the Gentiles should be compelled to keep the Law of Moses. There was considerable controversy over the matter, so it was decided that they would meet in Jerusalem to reach some agreement. Notice that in the fifteenth chapter of Acts, the apostle James addressed the matter. I shall not quote it all, but I want to underscore what he says, particularly beginning with the 19th verse. "Wherefore my sentence is, that we trouble not them, which from among the Gentiles are turned to God" (15:19).

If you have read more than the surface of the Scriptures, you will know that James was somewhat legally inclined. In other words, he was adamant about keeping the law and observances that had been given to Israel by Moses. James, the apostle, was not as generous with grace as Paul was. Therefore, it is significant to me that a man who appeared to have had a preference for bringing the Gentiles under the law could be moved and controlled by the Spirit of God to make the statement that he did. James suggested not placing any greater burden on them, "but that we write unto them, that they abstain from pollutions of idols, and from fornication, and from things strangled, and from blood" (Acts 15:20). Could any less have been required of the Gentiles? They could not permit the Gentiles to include idols in their worship, nor eat things strangled, nor drink the blood. The demands the apostles made on the Gentiles were at a bare minimum. The point I am making is this: the apostles were men, and had their own individual opinions. However, when they came together as servants of God, under the control of the Holy Spirit, they could suppress their own inclinations and preferences, and out of their conference would come the will of God. Apostolic doctrine and its practice is what I am talking about.

> It seemed good to the Holy Ghost, and to us, to lay upon you no greater burden than these necessary things; that ye abstain from meats offered to idols..., and from fornication: from which if ye keep yourselves, ye shall do well. (Acts 15:28-29)

They were men, and as humans, they were disposed to mistakes, but not under the control and direction of the Holy Ghost.

THE APOSTOLIC DESIRE

Let's examine Peter's experience in Antioch. He had been mingling freely with the Gentiles until certain men came up from Jerusalem. For a moment, Peter was just a man and was swayed by other men's attitudes. He began to back away from the Gentiles when the Jerusalem Jews were around. This is an example of the fallibility in man. The apostle Paul describes Peter's disaffection in the second chapter of his letter to the Galatians:

> But when I saw that they walked not uprightly according to the truth of the gospel, I said unto Peter before them all, if thou, being a Jew livest after the manner of Gentiles, and not as do the Jews, why compellest thou the Gentiles to live as do the Jews? (Galatians 2:14)

Paul, in the Spirit, reproved Peter's momentary wavering. Peter did not bristle at Paul's reproof and respond with, "I was in this before you," or "I walked with the Master personally." He did not cite his length of experience compared to Paul, and evidently took his rebuke in a spirit of humility. We can see from this encounter that the apostles were indeed men, but men under the control of the Holy Spirit which made all the difference in the world.

The apostles were in a position to set doctrine. If anybody should have understood what Jesus meant when He spoke, they should have. They walked with Him, ate with Him, heard His teachings, and caught His inflections. In addition, He had filled them with His spirit, and He had said to them, "The Holy Ghost...shall... bring all things to your remembrance" (John 14:26). Yes, undoubtedly, the apostles were in a position to set doctrine.

If anyone still objects to the apostles' doctrine and practices, be reminded that Jesus Himself left no written record for us to glean doctrine from. We have nothing that was personally written by Him. The only way to know what Jesus said is through these holy men Jesus Christ had appointed and commissioned. We can see then that we are absolutely dependent on them to tell us what Jesus said, and their interpretation either through the explanations they gave, or demonstrations that they set before us. What the apostles said and how they acted were merely their expressions of Jesus' words, so we can certainly be safe if we walk in the doctrine and practice of the apostles. Moreover, Jesus prayed that we should believe on Him through their (the apostles') word. In John 17:20, He prays, "Neither pray I for these alone, but for them also which shall believe on me through their word."

Throughout this chapter, I have attempted to establish that if we are to know what Jesus said and what He meant, then we must look at the doctrine and practice of the apostles.

~2~

GOD KEEPS HIS WORD

"I am the Lord, I change not".
Malachi 3:6

GOD DOES NOT CHANGE

There are so many denominations classified as Christian, all of which are divergent from one another, yet who are all professing to worship the same Lord. Remedies that were advocated for the ills that have beset us were rejected as being inadequate because we feel that the malady of professing Christendom has not been properly diagnosed. I positively believe that we are in this downhearted condition because we have left the original landmark and departed from apostolic doctrine and practices. In the beginning it was ever so gradual, but little by little, men started doing what they felt was right. At first, they hesitantly substituted a little of their opinion in place of the doctrine that was committed to us through the apostles. However, as the journey went on, the further away they drifted from God and oneness of faith until today, when every little group has its own private interpretation. Each has its own way of serving God—and they call it religious liberty.

We have been warned in the scriptures to take heed that our liberties do not become a stumbling block. But in spite of the warnings, that is exactly what has happened. We have wandered so far onto paths of our own, far from the original path, that if Jesus should arrive at this moment looking for the church that He established, He certainly would not recognize it in this conglomeration that we have on our hands. On one occasion when Jesus was teaching in a prophetic vein, He stopped and asked, "When the Son of man cometh, shall he find faith on the earth?" (Luke 18:8). Now that was a thought-provoking question! It was also a prophecy in the sense that when the Lord should come, things would have degenerated to the extent that genuine faith would be a scarce commodity. Jude exhorts us to "earnestly contend for the faith which was once delivered unto the saints" (Jude 1:3). I think that when Jesus comes to call His spirit-filled children, He will be looking for that one, true faith.

"Neither pray I for these alone, but for them also which shall believe on me through their word" (John 17:20). The prayer of Jesus, a request on behalf of those who shall believe on Him through the words of the apostles, signifies that the apostles were to be the authoritative interpreters of the word and the will of God in Christ Jesus. We should, therefore, carefully notice the utterances that Jesus gave forth which the Spirit brought to the apostles' remembrance, and we should further mark the manner in which they put the words which came forth from the lips of Jesus into practice. If we are careful and deeply concerned, there would be a genuine effort put forth to return to the faith which was once delivered to the saints. By no means am I advocating that everyone should come to me, nor should any denomination say, "Come to us." But this I do advocate: let us all return to that which we have strayed from, let us all seek out the doctrine and practices of the apostles, and let us try our very best to live accordingly. Our condition will be improved marvelously if we do.

LITERAL WORDS OF JESUS

Notice, the apostles took the words of Jesus literally when He spoke concerning the Holy Spirit—He is one and the same. Jesus said to the apostles, "And, behold, I send the promise of my Father upon you: but tarry ye in the city of Jerusalem, until ye be endued with power from on high." (Luke 24:49). This is a promise. He promised to them the assurance of the Father, and ordered them not to leave Jerusalem until they received that promise. Jesus knew fully well that in the strength, power, and wisdom of the flesh, the apostles did not have what was needed to propagate His doctrine. He knew what they would encounter in their attempts to spread His gospel and that is why He wisely cautioned them not to move until the power came. Jesus was, in effect, saying, "You cannot make it without me! But I will not leave you comfortless—I will come to you. Just don't go anywhere until I come." They took Jesus' promise literally.

> And he led them out as far as to Bethany, and he lifted up his hands, and blessed them. And it came to pass, while he blessed them, he was parted from them, and carried up into heaven. And they worshipped him, and returned to Jerusalem with great joy. (Luke 24:50-52)

The accounts of these acts are not the opinion of this author, they are written in the BOOK. Our only hope and salvation is in returning to the one true and original faith that was once delivered to the saints. Can you not see it? There is no choice here. If we want deliverance from the ills that plague us, we must return to the pristine purity of the Faith.

They "returned to Jerusalem with great joy." Notice, they had great joy, but the promise of the Father—the Holy Ghost—had not yet come. Just think of how many professing

Christians in the world today have made the mistake of jumping up and running when the joy came. They did not wait for the power! They experienced the joy when they were delivered from their sin and their burden of guilt was gone. But they left Jerusalem, so to speak, because they received the power. The apostles did not do this. THEY WAITED! Their joy was in anticipation of that which was yet to come. There was a promise to be fulfilled that Christ had made to them and they knew He would never lie to them. Their attitude was, "Our God cannot fail His promise; He told us to wait for Him, for He will return." So, the saints waited expectantly and confidently.

Wouldn't it be a wondrous occasion in professing Christendom today if everyone who heard of the call of God's sweet spirit would wait before His throne, and pray, trust, and look to Jesus until the promise of the Father should come to them? This is the example. God keeps His word. He does not promise a thing and fail to deliver, nor does He toy with men's souls. If He promised it, He will fulfill it, but you must meet His terms. One may ask the question: "Why don't many professing Christians possess the promise?" I think I can answer that question. They want the things that God gives them, but they forget what God instructs them to do. God told the blind man, "Go, wash in the pool of Siloam" (John 9:7). If that man had stood around wondering, asking himself, "What virtue is there in the pool of Siloam or what benefit can I get from washing my eyes?" he would have remained blind. However, when Jesus gave him something to do, HE DID IT. "He went his way therefore, and washed, and came seeing" (John 9:7).

Jesus said to the man with the withered hand, "Stand forth" (Mark 3:3). His hand would have stayed withered at his side if that man had refused to stand forth because he questioned the logic of Jesus' command by wondering, "What does Jesus mean to do, make a spectacle of me and my deformity?" But when Jesus said, "stand forth", he stepped forth by faith. Then Jesus gave him another command, to stretch out his hand. The man did not think, "Why would he tell me to foolishly stretch it out knowing that all these years I have not been able to do so?" If he had felt that way, absolutely nothing would have happened. But when he was told to stretch forth that hand, he attempted to do as he was commanded and realized that he now had the power to do so.

Do you realize now why we don't have the blessing of the Lord as we should? We are so dull from reasoning, logic, arguments, objections, and debate. All we have to do is obey God as they did in the days of old and we will receive what God gave them. "And when the day of Pentecost was fully come, they were all with one accord in one place" (Acts 2:1). Doing what? Doing what Jesus had said to do—waiting until the promise came.

> And suddenly there came a sound from heaven as of a rushing mighty wind, and it filled all the house where they were sitting, and there appeared unto them cloven tongues like as of fire, and it sat upon each of them. And they were all filled with the Holy Ghost, and began to speak with other tongues, as the Spirit gave them utterance. (Acts 2:2-4)

They had taken the Lord's promise concerning the Holy Spirit literally, and in their obedience to the things He had given them to do, they received the promise of the Father. Consider who was among those approximately one hundred twenty people that were filled with the Holy Spirit: Mary, the mother of Jesus (Acts 1:1-16). If she had lived in the modern age after having such a wonderful experience of birthing the world's Savior, she might have said, "Why do I need to tarry here—I have all I need—no one has ever been as blessed as I have. The Holy Spirit has overtaken me and I gave birth to the Son of God." But this was not so with Mary. Jesus told her, along with the others, to wait, and in obedience, that is what she did.

If you feel because of some special spiritual occurrence in your life that you do not need the promise of the Father, think again. You have never had an experience like Mary's, you've never walked on water as Peter did, you've never cast out devils or healed the sick quite as they did, nor have you opened the eyes of the blind. Other than what had happened to Mary, the apostles had done all of those things, and despite their wealth of experience and their wonderfully blessed association with Jesus, they remained in that upper room, WAITING. Waiting for what? The indispensable promise of the Father, which was the Holy Ghost—the power. They were not going to go anywhere until He came. Oh, that we would wait as they waited! Oh, that we would be as obedient!

If we would only obey and walk close to God as the apostles walked, we would have greater power, richer anointing, more abundant blessings, and much greater effectiveness with this gospel that we are supposed to preach. But man wants to ignore what God has told us to do. Consider Naaman, the Syrian, who had gone to Elisha for healing. After the man of God had instructed Naaman, he replied, "Are not Abana and Pharpar, rivers of Damascus, better than all the waters of Israel?" (2 King 5:12). Naaman, baffled by the prophet's request to dip seven times in the muddy waters of Jordan to be healed of leprosy, nearly walked away in disdain. Mark this well: he would have returned to Syria still a leper if it had not been for his servant who reasoned with him. The servant implored, "My father, listen, if the man of God instructed you to do some great things, wouldn't you have done it? How easy should it be to dip seven times in the Jordan? Go dip! What have you got to lose? Go do it." He saved Naaman from disobedience. And when Naaman obeyed and went down seven times into the muddy Jordan, "his flesh came again like unto the flesh of a little child, and he was clean" (2 King 5:10-14). What are we waiting for? Why not obey just as fully so that we might receive healing for our afflictions?

Now, the eleven apostles were in the first group that was filled with the Holy Ghost, but Paul also had to be filled when his heart was turned to God. He could not have been effective without the Holy Ghost. After Paul, known as Saul, had been knocked sprawling by the blinding light from heaven. he heard a voice saying, "Saul, Saul, why persecutest thou me?" (Acts 9:4). Saul said to the voice behind that blinding, terrifying light, "Who art thou, Lord?" And the voice continued, "I am Jesus whom thou persecutest: it is hard for thee to kick against the pricks" (Acts 9:5). Trembling and astonished, Paul said, "Lord, what wilt thou have me to do?" The Lord said unto him, "Arise, and go into the city, and it shall be told thee what thou must do" (Acts 9:5). Saul obeyed the Lord. He did not ask what would happen after he got into the city, nor did he ask why he should go there. He simply obeyed. It is so simple, yet very important to obey the voice of the Lord.

When Paul had gone into the city of Damascus, he stayed at the house of Judas, fasting and sightless for three days. God sent Ananias to pray for Paul at the right time. He said to Paul, "Brother Saul, the Lord, even Jesus, that appeared unto thee in the way as thou camest, hath sent me, that thou mightest receive thy sight and be filled with the Holy Ghost" (Acts 9: 17). And thus, it was so. Saul, the ravager of the church, was filled with the Spirit of God and became Paul the apostle—all because he obeyed.

Up to this point, I have ministered to you about how the Apostles took the Lord's commandments very seriously. They obeyed God completely and they received His Spirit within them. There was no doubt that the apostles had the Spirit of God with them because His power was manifested through them. Is the Spirit of God alive and active in you today?

~3~

THE APOSTOLIC THEME

"When the Day of Pentecost was fully come, they were all with one accord in one place...and they were all filled with the Holy Ghost, and began to speak with other tongues, as the Spirit gave them utterance."

Acts 2:1-4

ALL ON ONE ACCORD

According to various publications[3], some churches observe the second Sunday of June as the Day of Pentecost. I wonder how many of them really know what Pentecost means? I am not insinuating that readers of these publications are illiterate, incompetent, or that the general population is lacking in natural judgment, but I do wonder how many of them have experienced the essence of Pentecost in their heart.

My intention for the discussion of this subject is to be entirely objective, and it is my hope that each reader will be just as objective. In the course of dissecting this topic completely, it may be that I shall turn you around in the Scriptures quite merrily—but that is all right. Whatever I am sharing is not founded upon mythical whims or any desires of my own; IT IS FROM THE GOOD BOOK! I seek knowledge of the Holy Scriptures because I believe God meant for me to have it. Those whom He calls have a right to participate in His full blessings. Don't be reluctant to turn the pages of your Bible so that you might understand the wonderful promises of the Father. Be like the noble Bereans, who

---

"searched the scriptures daily, whether those things were so" (Acts 17:11).

THE BIBLICAL MESSAGE

In the preceding lesson, I attempted to establish certain points of apostolic principle and practice. First, the apostles indisputably accepted the words that Jesus spoke concerning the Holy Spirit. Secondly, the apostles obeyed the commandment of Jesus and received the promise of the Father. And now, with those points established, let us move to the third point, Jesus and the resurrection. The theme of apostolic preaching was Jesus and the resurrection. I am not talking about modern day preaching, I am referring to apostolic preaching. Present day teaching often tickles the ears and pleases the fancy, but it is not primarily concerned with the gospel. The holy men of the early church not only had the gospel, but they had the power of God because they were obedient to the commandment of Jesus Christ. They waited until the power came and when it did, their words were not so rhetorical. They were not orators, but beyond a shadow of a doubt, there was power in what they spoke. There was something in the words that they spoke when anointed by the Holy Ghost that connected to the hearts of men and moved them to action. These men and women who were so moved did not always obey the gospel, they did not always do what God wanted them to do, but they were moved.

Felix, the Roman governor, was one who was visibly moved. As Paul reasoned with Felix concerning the righteousness, temperance, and judgment to come, the Bible informs us that Felix trembled (Acts 23). There was a power in apostolic preaching that would cut men to their very souls.

It wasn't an occasional thing, but a consistent anointing that left men changed—saint or sinner.

At times, if they were sinners and did not surrender completely, it made them cry out. Even as Paul reasoned before Festus on one occasion, Festus cried out, "Paul, thou art beside thyself; much learning doth make thee mad" (Acts 26:24). He was telling Paul that he had gone insane, that he had lost his mind over religion. What was wrong with Festus? The words that Paul was speaking were going straight to the heart of both Agrippa and Festus, but neither one of them wanted to relinquish their set of beliefs. They did not feel that they could afford to give in to the doctrine that was being preached. Festus shook it off by saying that Paul had lost his mind, and Agrippa tried to use ridicule, saying to Paul, "Almost thou persuadest me to be a Christian" (Acts 26:28). However, both of those men, at that very hour, felt the power of the Word tug at their minds and their hearts. I long for the time when churches will go back to preaching the gospel as it was in the days of the apostles. It isn't that I am not opposed to training or preparation. I believe they are a vital part of the ministry. However, what a man needs most of all is preparation for the receiving of God's Holy Spirit. The spirit of the Lord should take control of the man—his mind, his utterance, his whole being. This is what we need to return to.

THE BOOK OF ACTS

The theme of the apostles' preaching was Jesus and the Resurrection. In the second chapter of Acts, we find an illustration of that memorable first sermon Peter preached on the Day of Pentecost. This was the very first sermon preached after the promise of the Father had been fulfilled (Acts 2:1-4). Peter was trying out the new equipment that

God had given to His messengers—a living tool—and he found that it was effectual and "a discerner of the thoughts and intents of the heart" (Hebrews 4:12). Further, Peter addressed the assembled multitude saying, "Ye men of Israel, hear these words; Jesus of Nazareth, a man approved of God among you by miracles and wonders and signs, which God did by him in the midst of you, as ye yourselves also know" (Acts 2:22). This passage is referring to Jesus having to be approved. He was to be the sacrifice for the sins of the world, a lamb without blemish, and without spot, so He had to be approved.

Moses was a great law giver, but he was not approved as a Savior. Abraham was the progenitor of the Jews, Jacob nicely fit as the head of the Israelites, and David was a great king out of the Tribe of Judah for Israel, but when it came to establishing a Savior, it had to be a lamb without spot or blemish in his life. He was a man approved by God. This was the message the apostles preached. Modern-day preachers often want to talk about a man who was merely great. Some say they doubt the virgin birth of Jesus, or doubt the Immaculate Conception. In fact, Jesus was a wonderful teacher and a revolutionary Rabbi. However, this is not an adequate recognition of Jesus because God gave him more. It was clear God approved Him because when Jesus spoke, God confirmed what He spoke by the miracles that were wrought. When He spoke, His speech was confirmed by signs and wonders. It was Jesus whom the apostles preached about, and it is the same Jesus whom we need to preach about today.

People are not wholeheartedly involved in the affairs of Jesus Christ and His full divinity as they ought to be. We are only dabblers in the truth. Some say, "Well now, it doesn't take all that much" and others say, "It doesn't matter so much whether He was virgin-born or not. He was a good man, so what is the difference?" I would reply that there is a difference. A good man cannot help you, a good man is unable to address your issue, and a good man can never fill your needs. We need someone who is divine! God is a spirit and He Himself has no body. Therefore, He took to Himself a body in the womb of a virgin, and then He came forth. He thus approved that body as sinless, spotless, and without blemish. It was not fathered by sinful flesh and thereby inherited none of mankind's sin. Afterward, God approved Him, and Peter later informed us that He was "delivered up" (Acts 3:13). Peter continues in Acts 2:23: "Him, being delivered by the determinate counsel and foreknowledge of God, ye have taken, and by wicked hands have crucified and slain."

This all had to be in the plan. It had to be a lamb that was offered—a sinless sacrifice. For if the sacrifice were not accepted, if it were not approved, and if something acceptable was not offered in our stead, we would have to die, and that would mean our eternal end. So first, Jesus had to be approved, and then he had to be offered up. But look! As Peter continues his sermon in verse 33 he says, "Therefore, being by the right hand of God exalted, and having received of the Father the promise of the Holy Ghost, he hath shed forth this, which ye now see and hear." Paul adds in his letter to the Romans that Jesus was "delivered up because of our offenses, and was raised because of our justification" (4:25).

Peter informed us that through His death and resurrection, Jesus was able to "shed forth this, which ye now see and hear." What was he talking about? He was talking about that which the multitude had pushed through the crowd to see and hear. When the Holy Ghost was poured out upon the approximately one hundred and twenty individuals in the upper room, they could not stay in that little room because the power on them was too great. Down they came into the street, staggering around like men who were drunk. Thus, the Scriptures were fulfilled: "They are drunken, but not with wine; they stagger, but not with strong drink" (Isaiah 29:9). They were reeling under the power of the Holy Spirit, speaking languages that they had never learned. It was such a remark-able sight that the multitude was amazed, and questions were exchanged back and forth. "What's the matter with these people?" Someone quipped, "I've got an explanation for it. They're full on new wine." Just about that time, Peter re-gained his composure. He no longer wanted to speak in tongues. He felt as Paul expressed: "In the church I had ra-ther speak five words with my understanding, that by my voice I might teach others also, than ten thousand words in an unknown tongue" (I Corinthians 14:19). In other words, he would rather have spoken in an understandable tongue so that listeners could comprehend the message he was bringing to them. After Peter had regained his equanimity, he said to the people looking on,

> For these are not drunken, as ye suppose, seeing it is but the third hour of the day. But this is that which was spoken by the prophet Joel; And it shall come to pass in the last days, saith God, I will pour out of my Spirit upon all flesh: and your sons and your daughters shall prophesy, and your young men shall see visions, and your old men shall dream dreams: and on my servants and my handmaidens I will pour out in those days of my Spirit; and they shall prophesy. (Acts 2:15-18)

Peter then went on in that notable sermon to tell them that Jesus, through his death and resurrection, has shed forth that which we all see and hear. It had never been like this in the world before. Whenever men had approached God in their sacrificial rituals, they had never experienced anything to compare with the happenings on that memorable Day of Pentecost. There is no evidence in the annals of history of such an occurrence before this one great day. God was doing a new thing, and a wonderful thing! One may say, "It's mighty foolish to cause men and women to speak in tongues." Maybe you would not have done things that way, dear reader, and it is possible that the wise men of the earth would have done it differently than God as well. But remember, "the foolishness of God is wiser than men" (1 Corinthians 1:25). God ordained the event of speaking in tongues, and because He did, that makes it all right with me. If anyone wishes that they could take all of their so-called wisdom, logic, and reasoning to do their own thing, and can establish their own plan of salvation, then well and good. If not, then they had better get in step with God's plan that was ordained before there was a world or men.

The apostle Peter explained the outpouring of the Holy Ghost to the multitude. In effect, he said that those men and women had been forgiven for their sins and filled with God's Holy Spirit; and this came about as a result of Jesus' death and resurrection, being raised up by the power divine. Not until Jesus had died on the cross and opened up heaven's windows to fully pardon all who would seek it—not until that time—was such a blessing, such a benefit made accessible.

Now, as Peter said, "Jesus hath shed forth this, which ye…see and hear." Peter continued his sermon. "Therefore, let all the house of Israel know assuredly, that God hath made that same Jesus, whom ye have crucified, both Lord and Christ" (Acts 2:36). In the preaching by the Apostles, they set forth the death of Christ as a substitute for your death and mine—for all who believe. They advocated the resurrection of Christ as our justification, making the Holy Spirit accessible to us. They also preached that by his supreme sacrifice, he was established as both Lord and Christ.

PETER'S SERMON

Next, let us consider Peter's sermon to the Gentiles found in the tenth chapter of the book of Acts. When God sent him to Cornelius, it was a new experience because Peter had never had any contact or dealings with the uncircumcised. However, God made it clear to Peter in a vision that he ought to go. He went in obedience to what God wanted, and he preached substantially the same sermon that was preached on the Day of Pentecost. Peter preached that Jesus Christ was God's anointed and that the spirit of the Living One was in Him, actuating, motivating, and sustaining Him. Acts 10:38 reads, "How God anointed Jesus of Nazareth with the Holy Ghost and with power: who went about doing good, and healing all that were oppressed of the devil; for God was with him." And just as he had on the Day of Pentecost, he went on to show that Jesus was crucified, that He was raised from the dead, and that He was appointed to deliver us from sin. Peter concludes in verses 39-41,

> And we are witnesses of all things which he did both in the land of the Jews, and in Jerusalem; whom they slew and hanged on a tree: Him God raised up the third day, and shewed him openly; Not to all the people, but unto witnesses chosen before of God, even to us, who did eat and drink with him after he rose from the dead.

Notice the next two verses. This is why the apostles refused to be stagnant about the promotion of the gospel:

> And he commanded us to preach unto the people, and to testify that it is he which was ordained of God to be the Judge of quick and dead. To him give all the prophets witness, that through his name

whosoever believeth in him shall receive remission of sins.

Peter made them aware that whatever they read from the prophets was referring to Jesus. The prophets were pointing to Jesus and notifying us, beforehand, that he was to come as the world's Savior.

Now, no one can have salvation in any other name. As Peter uttered on one occasion, "There is none other name under heaven given among men, whereby we must be saved" (Acts 4:12). Do you see what they preached? Do you see how they preached? It was Jesus and the Resurrection. They preached it wherever they went. Men and women believed it and were delivered from the bondage of sin. The church message today does not yield the results that the apostles' preaching did. One may ask, why? The answer is simple. Churches are not careful to preach the same doctrine that the apostles preached. We have left the *Apostolic Doctrine and Practice* and have come up with doctrines of our own: man-inspired sermons. Certainly, there is no question that those sermons are homiletically arranged, and they could meet today's standards, as far as theory goes. However, they fail to reach the hearts of sinners. They reach the ears, but not the heart.

On the Day of Pentecost, Peter preached Jesus and the Resurrection. The message cut to the heart of those same hard-hearted individuals that howled against Jesus and crucified Him. Such Holy Ghost preaching made them cry out, "Men and brethren, what shall we do?" (Acts 2:37). How often does modern-day preaching cause anyone to cry out? If one feels the need to cry out, it is usually because the individual is wearied with hearing so many palavers.

People stay away from churches in droves because they are not hearing the word of God. On Sunday mornings, some churches get through with the Lord in a hurry. Because they aren't able to draw in or keep people for very long, they have an early service and quickly get it over with for the day. Some churches have to close on Sunday nights when the weather gets hot because they cannot compete with air-conditioned theaters and other places of amusement. Let me tell you something: Dear brother, dear sister, if we get the power of God, we can draw in men and women even when it is a hundred degrees in the shade. If they have to wipe their brows, sweat, and fan, they will wipe their brows, sweat, and fan, and come back again and again. That is preaching as it was in the apostolic days. Jesus was the core of their message. He filled their hearts and motivated their lives. Jesus! Jesus! Jesus! He should be our theme today. An old song that we often sing, *Back to Pentecost*, comes to mind.

> I will not leave you comfortless
> But if I go away
> Will send the Holy Comforter
> Your royal guest forevermore
> Abiding day by day
> *Chorus:*
> Has he come to you, to you to you?
> Has the comforter come to you?
> The Lord will reprove the world of sin
> When the comforter comes to you.
> (Lelia Morris, 1938)

All men need the help of God! If we have it, we can make it, but if we don't have God's help, we are not fit for anything. Jesus said unto His disciples, "without me ye can do nothing" (John 15:5). That was true then and it is applicable today. Without God, we can do absolutely nothing. All of us need the Lord physically. We might have the will to do many good things, but if we do not have His supernatural power to carry on, it would be as Jesus spoke to His disciples: "the spirit indeed is willing, but the flesh is weak" (Matthew 26:41). Likewise, we need Him for spiritual power and direction.

In that regard, I am so glad that I learned to trust the Lord. The Lord taught me that if I would only put my trust in Him, everything would be all right. I can say very personally that I am not bothered about not having money because I do not worry about the material things of life. As long as Jesus leads me, that is all I need—for he satisfies completely. There is a more important necessity of life beyond the material needs, and without it, we would be lacking. That necessity that I have been talking about throughout this writing is divine unction. Dear reader, that divine power, that element that makes the difference between the word of man and the Word of God, is called the UNCTION OF THE LORD. Hypothetically, imagine an individual memorizing the sermon that the apostle Peter preached to the public on the Day of Pentecost—every syllable. Imagine that this person that has taken public speaking and oratory lessons. After they felt confident enough to go out and face an audience with that same sermon, I dare say that they would not create one little ripple of excitement among that audience. They certainly could not create a real deep, moving repentance in a sinful heart. The effect of Peter's sermon was not in the words that he spoke, it was in the anointing that God gave.

Mark this well: words themselves mean nothing, and it is only when God anoints them that they become "quick, and powerful, and sharper than any twoedged sword, piercing even to the dividing asunder of soul and spirit, and of the joints and marrow, and...a discerner of the thoughts and intents of the heart" (Hebrews 4:12). Consequently, if we want to have effective preaching and power behind our message, we need to go back to the apostolic teaching and practices.

Previously, I discussed Peter's sermon on the Day of Pentecost and the sermon he delivered to the household of Cornelius. Now, I want you to look at another preacher of apostolic times and examine his message. You will see that they all did the same thing and spoke with the same theme because Jesus filled their thoughts. Jesus not only possessed their minds, He controlled their movements and that is the reason they were so effective. If we want to deal with men's souls and not only their minds, we are going to have to find the gospel that is effective. The apostle Paul shared in his letter to the Romans (1:16) that the gospel of Jesus Christ is, "The power of God unto salvation to every one that believeth; to the Jew first, and also to the Greek [Gentile]" (1:16).

PHILIP'S OBEDIENCE

Our example is the apostle Philip, the evangelist. He showed us evidence of the total submission that they all displayed; the point at which someone realizes that God is everything and they are nothing. When God spoke, the desires of the apostles were completely overruled. Acts 8:26 reads: "And the angel of the Lord spake unto Philip, saying, Arise, and go toward the south unto the way that goeth down from Jerusalem unto Gaza, which is desert." What I like about this statement is the detailed way God can direct people when there is complete acquiescence to His will. However, you will not receive that same divine control and direction if you have grand ideas that you want to accomplish. One must be careful to not have a personal agenda in God's way. "And he arose and went" (Acts 8:27).

Philip had been engaged in a wonderful revival in Samaria where the sick were healed, demons were cast out, and the lame made to walk. There was joy throughout the city because multitudes had believed and were baptized in the name of the Lord Jesus. But in the midst of such wonderful events, the spirit of the Lord had been able to seize Philip's attention.

Oh, to develop such an attitude that no matter what goes on around us, God can get our attention! If you pay attention to the voices of unbelievers, you can lose your soul. If you observe the attitudes of mere men and women, you will miss the mind of God completely. In order for the messengers to do what God says, reasonable or unreasonable, they must be in a state of full surrender to God. Oh God, grant it to us more and more as the days wear on. Philip left Samaria, as God had directed, and traveled along the way leading from Jerusalem to Gaza.

> And, behold, a man of Ethiopia, a eunuch of great authority under Candace queen of the Ethiopians, who had the charge of all her treasure, and had come to Jerusalem for to worship, was returning, and sitting in his chariot reading Esaias the prophet. Then the Spirit said unto Philip, Go near and join thyself to this chariot (Acts 8:27-29).

There are those who say, "God does not speak today," and this is my reply: God speaks, but we just don't listen. We listen to everybody but the Lord. We hear the babble of the multitude and then we say that He no longer talks as in the days of old. God has not lost His power of speech. He can and will talk if you can hear. No individual will make a good minister of Jesus Christ if they cannot hear the voice of the Lord. If they cannot unmistakably feel the leading of God's Spirit—not necessarily through a light, a literal vision or a thundering voice—they will never make a good minister. It may be a still voice, deep within the soul, but one so positive that the messenger cannot miss it.

> And Philip ran thither to him, and heard him read the prophet Esaias, and said, Understandest thou what thou readest? And he said, How can I, except some man should guide me? And he desired Philip that he would come up and sit with him. (Acts 8:30-31)

The passage of scripture that he read was,

> He was led as a sheep to the slaughter; and like a lamb dumb before his shearer, so opened he not his mouth: in his humiliation his judgement was taken away: and who shall declare his generation? For his life is taken from the earth. (Acts 8:32-33)

Note the perfect timing when God chose to gain the ear of His servant. Notice the operation and synchronization through which God was able to lead His servant by His Holy Spirit. Philip found this man alone in a desert and the two of them were brought together in that wasteland because Philip allowed the Holy Spirit to lead him. By obeying the leading of the Lord, Philip arrived at the right time to hear the eunuch reading a scripture that would provide a text for his sermon. Subsequently, the eunuch answered Philip, "I pray thee, of whom speaketh the prophet this? of himself, or of some other man? Then Philip opened his mouth, and began at the same scripture, and preached unto him Jesus" (Acts 8:34-35).

JESUS, THE RESURRECTION

As previously established, the theme of apostolic preaching was Jesus and the Resurrection. Philip had no personal philosophy, nor did he quote any great men of the day. He began at the same scripture, and preached unto him, Jesus. When considering this passage, we should not imagine that Philip just said, "Jesus! Jesus! Jesus!" Jesus was the theme, but we can discern the substance of the message from the reaction of the one preached to. Philip was engrossed in his message about Jesus and the Resurrection. After reading the words "He was led as a sheep to the slaughter," he certainly would have preached that Jesus was the sacrifice the world needed, the offering for sin, and that His blood would save all that believed in Him. Further, Philip must have mentioned water baptism. I offer this evidence: When the eunuch saw a body of water out in the desert, he said, "See, here is water; what doth hinder me to be baptized?" (Acts 8:36).

Let me make another point before I conclude this writing. The apostles sought believers to understand and to receive the promise of God. They knew that a profession of faith in Jesus Christ was the assent of the mind, however, they did not want believers to stop with a work performed only at the surface. I could not be satisfied with men and women flocking into the church that I pastor saying, "I believe! I believe!" and then going back to their seats. That would never satisfy me. I want to know that something effective is wrought in them. Something must happen in those individuals that will give them the power to live for Christ. My spirit cannot rest with you merely being a professor. I want a blood-washed Christian to be totally submitted to the Lord. And that is what the apostles wanted in their day.

Once again, we shall look at the second chapter of the Acts of the Apostles. We have gone there often, yet it provides examples and that is what the word of the Lord is for. This matter is somewhat controversial and because it is, be sure to stick close to your Bible and forget what you like, what you have heard, and what you have thought. It reads,

> Now when they heard this, they were pricked in
> their heart, and said unto Peter and to the rest of the

apostles, Men and brethren, what shall we do? Then Peter said unto them, Repent and be baptized every one of you in the name of Jesus Christ for the remission of sins, and ye shall receive the gift of the Holy Ghost. For the promise is unto you, and to your children, and to all that are afar off [including us], even as many as the Lord our God shall call. (Acts 2:37-39)

Notice verse 41: "Then they that gladly received his word were baptized: and the same day there were added unto them about three thousand souls." Some have asserted that they were added simply by baptism, but I do not believe that. What would it have taken to add them? In verse 4 of the same chapter, we read that the approximately one hundred and twenty souls (Acts 1:15) spoke with other tongues: "And they were all filled with the Holy Ghost, and began to speak with other tongues, as the Spirit gave them utterance." Therefore, if the original group spoke with other tongues, in order for the new converts (three thousand) to be added unto them, they had to have had the same experience.

Now take notice of Acts 8:14-15, which recounts a time before Philip had left Samaria to meet the eunuch, and observe the reaction of the apostles to the revival Philip was conducting in Samaria. "When the apostles which were at Jerusalem heard that Samaria had received the word of God, they sent unto them Peter and John: who, when they were come down, prayed for them, that they might receive the Holy Ghost."

Do you see what I see? The apostles were not content that these Samaritans should just make a profession, nor were they satisfied with a mere assent of the mind. They wanted a deep work wrought in these new believers. Let me remind you that wonderful things had taken place in Samaria. The infirmed were healed, the lame began walking, and demons had been cast out, but it wasn't enough. They had to give themselves up completely to God and be led by his Spirit. "For as many as are led by the Spirit of God, they are the sons of God" (Romans 8:14). It is not my intention to be repetitious, but it is necessary for me to make a point. When those who were in Jerusalem heard that the word of God had been wonderfully received at Samaria, they sent unto them Peter and John, who prayed for them that they might receive the Holy Ghost. They had received the baptism in Jesus' name, but the Holy Ghost had not fallen upon any of them. "Then they laid their hands on them, and they received the Holy Ghost" (Acts 8:14-17). Now, some may pause here and say, But the scripture doesn't say that they spoke with other tongues. Are you a reasonable person? What on earth was left for them to do? Demons had been cast out, the sick had been healed, they had great joy, and they had been baptized in the name of the Lord Jesus, but they had not yet reached that point of total submission. Peter and John prayed for them and they received the Holy Ghost. I sincerely believe that they spoke with other tongues as the Spirit gave them utterance.

Continuing in the same passage, here is another strong point. We are told in the scriptures that one by the name of Simon, the sorcerer (Acts 8:9), had been in Samaria where Philip was ministering before the arrival of Peter and John on the scene. He had never offered to buy anything from Philip, yet when the two apostles arrived, Simon came and saw the gift of the Holy Ghost come upon the people, then out came his money pouch and he made an offer to buy that power. He said, "Give me also this power, that on whomsoever I lay hands, he may receive the Holy Ghost" (Acts 8:19). Dear reader, this is my question to you: what was it that he heard? He heard that same marvelous thing that they heard at the household of Cornelius (Acts 10). He heard that same marvelous thing they heard at Ephesus when Paul encountered a group of disciples that had not yet received the Holy Ghost, nor had ever heard that there was such a thing as the Holy Ghost (Acts 19:1-7). Simon heard them as they "[spoke] with tongues" (Acts 10:46).

God has given this as a sign of one's total submission. Peter said, "We are [his] witnesses" (Acts 10:39). So, when you reach that point of total submission, you will speak with tongues. Some may counter, "Well, I don't think you ought to go seeking tongues." Was anything said about seeking tongues? The apostles were not in the upper room seeking tongues, they were waiting for the promise of the Father. And when the promise came, they spoke. Therefore, you do not need to seek anything but that point of total submission to God, and when He comes, He will speak through you. May the Lord bless you.

HYMN I

BACK TO PENTECOST

I will not leave you comfortless
But if I go away
Will send the Holy Comforter
Your royal guest forevermore
Abiding day by day

Chorus:
Has he come to you, to you to you?
Has the comforter come to you?
The Lord will reprove the world of sin
When the comforter comes to you.

(Lelia Morris, 1938)

HYMN II

HOLY SPIRIT, LIGHT DEVINE

Holy Ghost with light divine
Shine upon this heart of mine.
Chase the shades of night away
Turn my darkness into day

Holy Ghost with power divine
Cleanse this guilty heart of mine.
Long hath sin without control
Held dominion o'er my soul.

Holy Ghost with joy divine
Cheer this saddened heart of mine.
Bid my many woes depart
Heal my wounded, bleeding heart.

(*Hymnal of the Methodist Episcopal Church*, 1881)

EPILOGUE

"**G**od said it and that settles it!" as the old adage goes. *Apostolic Doctrine and Practice* sought to highlight the fact that Christians today have drifted far away from the original landmark of Christianity that was established by Jesus Christ and upheld by His apostles. We have strayed from the intention of the testimony of the apostle Paul, "One Lord, one faith, one baptism, one God and Father of all, who [is] above all, and through all, and in you all" (Ephesians 4:5-6) to a plurality of denominations. Nowhere does Scripture mandate denominationalism; to the contrary, the mandate is for unity. In fact, history conveys that denominationalism is caused by conflict and confrontation which leads to division and separation. Jesus said that a house divided against itself cannot stand. This general principle can and should be applied to the church. We find an example in the Corinthian church where members were struggling with issues of division and separation. There were those who thought that they should follow Paul and those who thought they should follow the teaching of Apollos.

> Now this I say, that every one of you saith, I am of Paul; and I of Apollos; and I of Cephas; and I of Christ. Is Christ divided? was Paul crucified for you? or were ye baptized in the name of Paul? (1 Corinthians 1:12-13)

These verses alone should tell us what Paul thought of denominations or anything that separated and divided the body of Christ. But let's look further. In verse 13, Paul asks very pointed questions: Is Christ divided? Was it Paul who was crucified for you? Or were you baptized in Paul's name? This makes how Paul felt very clear. He (Paul) was not the Christ, he was not the one who was crucified and his message has never been intended to divide the church or lead someone to worship Paul instead of Christ. Obviously, according to Paul, there is only one church and one body of believers and anything that is different weakens and destroys the church (1 Corinthians 1:17).

As we look at church organizational separations today, disagreement over the interpretation of Scripture has become a leading issue. These disagreements are taken personally and become points of contention. This leads to arguments which can and have done much to destroy the witness of the church. The church should be able to resolve its differences inside the body, but once again, history tells us that this often doesn't happen. Scripture says,

> Do ye not know that the saints shall judge the world? And the world shall be judged by you, are ye unworthy to judge the smallest matters? Know ye not that we shall judge angels? How much more things that pertain to this life? (1 Corinthians 6:2-3)

Denominations are used by man out of self-interest. There are denominations today that are in a state of self-destruction as they are being led into apostasy by those who are promoting their personal agendas instead of God's agenda. Today the media uses our differences against us to demonstrate that we are not unified in thought or purpose. As church leaders, we must lay aside our personal agenda and seek out God's agenda through Scripture less we find ourselves wrestling the Word of God to our own peril as the Pharisees.

What is a believer to do? Should we ignore denominations, should we just not go to church and worship on our own at home? The answer to both questions is no. What we should be seeking is a body of believers where the Gospel of Christ is preached as by the apostles, where you as an individual can have a personal relationship with the Lord, where you can join in biblical ministries that are spreading the Gospel and glorifying God. Attending church is important, and all believers need to belong to a body that fits the above criteria. We need relationships that can only be found in the body of believers, we need the support that only the church can offer, and we need to serve God in the community as well as individually. As believers, we must return to the basics of the Word of God. We must believe, preach, and teach the words of Jesus as done by the apostles.

The substance of this book deals with various matters that are somewhat controversial. While I do not delight in controversy, to be faithful in my calling I must, at times, come into conflict with opinions that are contrary to the Word of the Lord. God forbid that some would be so averse to differences of opinion that they shun declaring the whole counsel of God.

AUTHOR

On October 5, 1892, a fourth child named Karl Franklin was born to Henry and Mary Smith in Zanesville, Ohio in their home on Fisher Street, located on Putnam Hill. His parents were both ministers of the African Methodist Church. As a child, Karl contracted scarlet fever before he was four years old. This situation constituted a serious threat to his life as no cure had yet been found to combat scarlet fever at that time. Nevertheless, God had a mission for his life that could not be hindered. Though common as it was, the birth of this child was to have extraordinary developments where God was concerned. Whether through divine intervention or natural means it isn't quite certain, however, Karl's life was spared.

Around the year 1912, Karl attended a service one night where his mother was conducting revival services in Cleveland, Ohio. That night he felt the hand of God upon him, prompting him to publicly confess Jesus Christ as his Savior. Shortly afterward Karl accepted the call of God on his life to become a minister of the Gospel. It seemed to be good news when Karl told his mother about his call to the ministry although she had not really wanted him to go in that direction, despite what might be termed his ministerial heritage. Perhaps it was that she wanted to protect him from the hardships that surrounded the life of a minister.

Karl enrolled into Payne Theological Seminary at Wilberforce University to prepare himself for his career. While in his second year of seminary, Karl took charge as temporary pastor over a small Mission in Columbus, Ohio. His assignment would last for only six months but would bring him in contact with the Edwards family who were filled with the Holy Ghost, evidenced by speaking in other tongues. They had been devout Methodists until some of the people from an apostolic faith church began witnessing to them. Mother Edwards tried to win Karl to her new apostolic views. She wanted him to denounce his Methodist baptism and accept baptism in the name of Jesus Christ and speaking in other tongues. Secretly, he began to search the Scriptures to learn more about the apostolic faith. At the end of an emotional journey during which he had to admit to his own stubbornness and the preemptive demands of a sovereign God, he was filled with the baptism of the Holy Ghost, speaking in other tongues on April 18, 1915.

In 1916, Karl settled in the city of Columbus, Ohio and made it his permanent home. He began attending a church pastored by Elder Robert C. Lawson and lived a few years with his pastor. In September 1915, Karl was ordained an elder in the Pentecostal Assemblies of the World. Shortly afterward, he met Josephine Jackson. They became engaged and on December 4, 1915 they were married. Soon thereafter, Karl Smith became the assistant pastor to Elder Lawson. Elder Smith held several important positions in the Pentecostal ranks. In 1919, he became the pastor of the Columbus church after Elder Lawson resigned and became the first general secretary of the Refuge Churches of Christ of the Apostolic Faith in 1920.

In 1941 Karl Smith launched the beginning of Aenon Bible School, the official educational institution of the Pentecostal Assemblies of the World, Inc. One of his most valuable resources however, was listening to every well-qualified Bible teacher he could. Bishop G.T. Haywood would make, by far, the greatest impression on him. To Karl F. Smith, all that mattered was the will of God, even if it called for his own personal distress. So, he endured the inconveniences of failing health, and bore its concomitant misery and pain with the stoic demeanor of one who has committed all his ways to God. God could not wait so that His servant could see the fruition of years of labor at Aenon Bible College. In His wisdom and sovereignty, He decreed that the journey was over, and He called him home on January 25, 1972.

CPSIA information can be obtained
at www.ICGtesting.com
Printed in the USA
BVHW030830311021
619709BV00004B/1